RACHE

PRAYING
the Psalms

31 DAYS OF BARING GRIEF BEFORE GOD

BIBLE READING PLAN & JOURNAL

PPRAYING THE PSALMS
ible Reading Plan and Journal
Published by Rachel Wojo
Copyright © 2020 by Rachel Wojnarowski

Visit rachelwojo.com/shop

Requests for information should be addressed to
rachel@rachelwojo.com
DIGITAL DOWNLOAD

Cover design by Rachel Wojo

Cover Credit: Rachel Wojo
Library of Congress Cataloging-in-Publication Data
Printed in the United States of America
2020

A Personal Note from Rachel

Dear Friend,

When I lost my mama to leukemia twenty years ago, my husband encouraged me to read the Psalms. The book of Psalms became a familiar friend, one that I would spend time with over and over again, pouring balm on my hurting heart.

When deep loss struck again and my daughter, Taylor, went to heaven, the book of Psalms became more than a familiar friend. I felt the depth of the words in my soul on a level that I can't explain. The emotional tie grew deeper than friendship; it became a blood bond.

In the days following Taylor's funeral, I would drop off my children to school and return home to an empty house. Sorrow would roll over my soul and I wept. I couldn't think rationally. I found myself pouring over the psalms again. For as long as it took to gain enough strength to get up and do what I had to do next. Whether I needed to sweep the floor or write an article, I somehow could find enough clarity and strength in the psalms to get through the next moment. The next day, it all repeated. I'm still reading at least one psalm daily and imagine I will do so for the rest of my life.

Praying the Psalms provides strength that I can't explain. The lyrics don't hold back in their intensity. Whether in joy or sorrow, the integrity of the psalms is captivating. The particular chapters chosen for this Bible reading plan and journal focus on prayer to God.

No matter your circumstances, my prayer for you is that you find this plan to be a gracious guide to the healing and mercy of the Psalms. May it surge over you daily as you attempt to move forward.

Thanks for joining me!
Rachel

Daily Guide

TO GROW YOUR FAITH

STEP 01   Have a conversation with God, asking him to help you read and understand his Word.

STEP 02   Read the Bible passage for the day one time slowly, soaking in each phrase. Read again if time allows.

STEP 03   Follow the guide to complete the journal sections.

Why Pray the Psalms?

God loves it when we pray His Word back to Him for multiple reasons. He loves that we know His Word well enough to pray it back to Him and He loves that we believe His Word. But what about the book of Psalms is so special?

Maybe the book of Psalms isn't any more special than any other book of the Bible, but we are drawn to the transparent honesty of the writers, especially David.

I read the book of Psalms several times in my early twenties. Honestly, I found it to be beautiful, but that depth of beauty equaled my experience and maturity level.

When deep sorrow entered my world and heart, I could feel the depth of the psalmists' sorrows. Before that, I didn't quite get it. In my deepest pain, I had the opportunity to experience God's deepest love.

I want to share with you that the prayers I've included in this book are real. They have been wrought in mourning and heartache. This may not be the right time for you to read raw prayers of grief. But you'll know when it is. And that's why you should pray the Psalms.

A PRAYER FOR MERCY

Day 1

READ

Psalm 4:1-8

PRAY

God, I need answers. You are the God of righteousness and I need You to hear my prayer. Please give me relief from my distress. I need Your mercy and grace. Let my community seek You alone. Let me be the example of Your faithfulness as others see my prayers answered. I know You hear me when I call to You. Help me to search my own heart and be judgment-free toward others. Give me full trust in You. Bless my community, Lord. Let the light of Your face shine on those in my circle of influence and fill me with joy at the sight of Your provision. It is because of You that I can rest my head on the pillow at night, Father. You alone make me safe.

REFLECT

Which verse or phrase from the psalm is emphasized in your heart today?

_____

_____

_____

_____

REWRITE

Use phrases from the psalm, prayer or reflection above to write out your prayer to God.

_____

_____

_____

_____

REMEMBER GRATITUDE

Does the psalmist give thanks? If so, for what? If not, why do you think it is left out?

_____

_____

_____

_____

_____

_____

_____

_____

_____

_____

Father, I need Your mercy and grace.

REACH FORWARD

It seems that when the psalmist takes his eyes off of his own issues and looks on the needs of others, he experiences some relief from his pain. Who could you pray for right now? Maybe someone you know in need or a situation out of control. Is there anything God would have you to do that would help the issue?

_____

_____

_____

_____

_____

A PRAYER FOR GUIDANCE

Day 2

READ

Psalm 5:1-12

PRAY

Lord, I need You to listen to my words. I need You to consider my sorrow and answer my cry for help, for it is to You alone I pray. I know You hear my voice and this morning, I lay my requests before You. I know You will answer them and I wait in expectation. I know that You are not pleased with sin and pride cannot stand in Your presence. You hate sin, but You love sinners. Thank You for loving me and thank You for the privilege of entering into Your presence through Your great love. Lead me in Your way; don't let the enemy trip me up through evil influences, I leave the evil to Your discretion and take refuge in You. Fill my heart with gladness and let me sing for joy.

REFLECT

Which verse or phrase from the psalm is emphasized in your heart today?

_____

_____

_____

_____

REWRITE

Use phrases from the psalm, prayer or reflection above to write out your prayer to God.

_____

_____

_____

_____

REMEMBER GRATITUDE

Does the psalmist give thanks? If so, for what? If not, why do you think it is left out?

_____

_____

_____

_____

_____

_____

_____

_____

_____

_____

*Lord, I need You
to guide me.*

REACH FORWARD

David encountered many enemies over the course of his life. He recognized that the enemies were not just his enemies, but God's enemies. He saw them for their lies and hatred, but did not seek to take matters in his own hands without God's approval. How could you pray for your enemy today? How might this help you experience the guidance you need?

_____

_____

_____

_____

_____

A PRAYER FOR MERCY

Day 3

READ

Psalm 39:12&13

PRAY

Lord, please hear my prayer. Open your ears to my desperation. Listen to my cry for help; hear my pleas for help. The grief flooding my heart is too much for me. I feel isolated and lonely in a world full of people. It doesn't seem as though I fit in anywhere. Everything feels foreign and strange; I'm unsure what to do about it. Lord, help me to enjoy life again. Forgive me and remove the shame I feel in Your presence. Relieve me from the burdens because I don't think I can take any more; everything inside of me is dying. You are my only Hope.

REFLECT

Which verse or phrase from the psalm is emphasized in your heart today?

_____

_____

_____

_____

REWRITE

Use phrases from the psalm, prayer or reflection above to write out your prayer to God.

_____

_____

_____

_____

REMEMBER GRATITUDE

Does the psalmist give thanks? If so, for what? If not, why do you think it is left out?

_____

_____

_____

_____

_____

_____

_____

_____

_____

Father, I need the relief that only You can give.

REACH FORWARD

The verses in today's passage are the closing or "interlude" to the bigger picture of Psalm 39. David begins the psalm by describing his battle with his own tongue. He explains his inner turmoil with using his words appropriately and controlling his temper. How much of our grief is the result of our own actions? What preventive measure could you take to prevent a problem from occurring?

_____

_____

_____

_____

_____

Day 4

READ

Psalm 69:1-12

PRAY

God, save me from the waves that threaten to drown me. There is no place for my feet to stand steady. I have come into deep waters and the floods engulf my soul. I'm worn out with calling out for help; I can't ask anymore. I'm trying to see you, Lord, but I can't. The number of my enemies is greater than my friends. I've failed you, Lord, and I know that You can see it. Please don't let me disgrace You. Don't let my mistakes prevent others from seeing who You really are. Though I am persecuted and laughed at, though I am misunderstood and insulted, let my trust remain in You alone.

REFLECT

Which verse or phrase from the psalm is emphasized in your heart today?

_____

_____

_____

_____

REWRITE

Use phrases from the psalm, prayer or reflection above to write out your prayer to God.

_____

_____

_____

_____

REMEMBER GRATITUDE

Does the psalmist give thanks? If
so, for what? If not, why do you
think it is left out?

_____

_____

_____

_____

_____

_____

_____

_____

_____

_____

*Father, may my mistakes
never prevent others
from seeing You.*

REACH FORWARD

David's honest writing is appealing when you've experienced the depths
of despair. His raw frankness reminds us to speak truth before our God,
as He is the only One who knows our hearts. Have you ever made a
mistake out of zeal? Your passion perhaps caused a problem in a
ministry or church? David admitted his imperfections and asked God to
protect others from losing sight of God's power. Use this section to write
a prayer to God on behalf of those you influence, that your mistakes
might not hinder their perspective of God.

_____

_____

_____

_____

_____

Day 5

READ

Psalm 69:13-18

PRAY

Lord, I pray to You that at the exact right time in Your unfailing love that You would answer me and save me. Rescue me, Lord, from the muck; don't let me sink into despair. Deliver me from the deepest waters that threaten to overtake me. Whether the waves threaten to flood over me or the riptide threatens to pull me under, don't let me drown. Lord, out of Your love and mercy, reveal Yourself and answer me. Come near me and rescue me because the enemy is great.

REFLECT

Which verse or phrase from the psalm is emphasized in your heart today?

_____

_____

_____

_____

REWRITE

Use phrases from the psalm, prayer or reflection above to write out your prayer to God.

_____

_____

_____

_____

REMEMBER GRATITUDE

Does the psalmist give thanks? If so, for what? If not, why do you think it is left out?

_____

_____

_____

_____

_____

_____

_____

_____

_____

_____

* * * * * * * * * * * * * * * * * * * *

Lord,
at Your perfect time.

* * * * * * * * * * * * * * * * * * *

REACH FORWARD

Even in the depths of despair, David prays for God's perfect timing. (v. 13) I think I often go to God as a toddler, stomping my feet and asking for whatever it is, "right now." Maybe you too? What part of your attitude could you change in your prayer?

_____

_____

_____

_____

_____

A PRAYER OF REMEMBRANCE

Day 6

READ

Psalm 143:1-6

PRAY

Lord, hear my prayer. I need your mercy. You are faithful and You are righteous. In appeal to these traits, I ask You for mercy. No one is perfect but You. The enemy chases after me and crushes me. He wants nothing more than to see me so deep in the darkness that I am dead. If he can exhaust my spirit and dismay my heart, then he is happy to prevent me from doing Your will. So I remember that You are the Creator of the world. Since the beginning of time, Your works are unfathomable. I stand before You with open hands, longing to receive what only You can give. I long to soak up all that You offer.

REFLECT

Which verse or phrase from the psalm is emphasized in your heart today?

_____

_____

_____

_____

REWRITE

Use phrases from the psalm, prayer or reflection above to write out your prayer to God.

_____

_____

_____

_____

REMEMBER GRATITUDE

Does the psalmist give thanks? If
so, for what? If not, why do you
think it is left out?

_____

_____

_____

_____

_____

_____

_____

_____

_____

_____

*Lord, I remember
all that Your hands
have created.*

REACH FORWARD

It's easy to be so stuck in the moment that you can think of nothing else
but the current situation or circumstances. David explains the deep
depression of his soul in today's psalm, but he also shares what helped
him get out of the deep pit of despair. He began to remember God's
history, from the beginning of time to God's work in his own life. These
thoughts of who God is and what He is capable of spurred David to think
of the potential. He positioned himself to receive the blessings of the
future. What stories of God's work come to your mind that would help
you open yourself to the possibilities of the future?

_____

_____

_____

_____

_____

A PRAYER OF TRUST

Day 7

READ

Psalm 143:7-12

PRAY

Lord, I need an answer quickly. I'm losing it and I need to see Your work in my life. Without it, I'm ready to die. Show me a new glimpse of Your unfailing love. I trust You, God. Show me the way to go; I have given you my life. Rescue me from the enemy; You are my hiding place. Teach me Your way and Your will, Lord. May Your good spirit lead me in a place, where the ups and downs of life have been levelled. Preserve my life that it is used for Your glory. Bring me out of trouble through Your righteousness and in Your unfailing love, hush the enemies' mouth. I am Your servant and I know that You have the victory.

REFLECT

Which verse or phrase from the psalm is emphasized in your heart today?

_____

_____

_____

_____

REWRITE

Use phrases from the psalm, prayer or reflection above to write out your prayer to God.

_____

_____

_____

_____

REMEMBER GRATITUDE

Does the psalmist give thanks? If
so, for what? If not, why do you
think it is left out?

_____

_____

_____

_____

_____

_____

_____

_____

_____

_____

*I trust You, Lord;
show me the way.*

REACH FORWARD

In verse 8, David emphasizes the relief that a morning can bring. You
never know what can happen in a day. I realize that can be positive or
negative, but David anticipates that the morning is going to reveal God's
unfailing love. What could you do to train your eye to seek a peek of the
blessings in the midst of heartache and pain? Perhaps keep a journal?
Make a "blessings" photo album on your phone?

_____

_____

_____

_____

_____

A PRAYER OF DECLARATION

Day 8

READ

Psalm 55:16-23

PRAY

God, I call to You. No matter who or what everyone else turns to, I turn to You because You save me. No matter the time of day, I cry out to You in my distress and You hear my voice. You rescue me without even a scratch in the midst of the battle. You have sat on the throne since the beginning of time and You do not change. You humble those who have no fear of You. When I give my burdens to You, You sustain me. When my heart aligns with Yours, I am not shaken. Though evil can seem to have the upper hand, God, You are still in control. As for me, I trust in You.

REFLECT

Which verse or phrase from the psalm is emphasized in your heart today?

_____

_____

_____

_____

REWRITE

Use phrases from the psalm, prayer or reflection above to write out your prayer to God.

_____

_____

_____

_____

REMEMBER GRATITUDE

Does the psalmist give thanks? If so, for what? If not, why do you think it is left out?

_____

_____

_____

_____

_____

_____

_____

_____

_____

_____

*Lord, as for me,
I trust in You.*

REACH FORWARD

David knows that his faith in God is contrary to the beliefs of many others, even some in his close circle. So he boldly declares in verse 16 of Psalm 55, "as for me" and repeats it in verse 23, "But as for me.," because no matter what everyone else is doing and no matter how everyone else sees things, David's trust and confidence is in the Lord. What if you simply labelled all the obstacles that the enemy wants to use in your life and declared to the Lord, "but as for me?"

_____

_____

_____

_____

_____

A PRAYER OF BLESSING

Day 9

READ

Psalm 67:1-7

PRAY

God, be gracious to me and bless me. Let the light of Your face shine on me, that I would be a clear reflection of You. Let Your ways be known on the earth. Show Your saving grace throughout the earth. May my life, my family, and my community bring praise to You. May people everywhere praise You, Lord, and recognize who You are. Let the song of joy begin in my heart, for You are just and true. May the song spread to others around me, bringing You praise. I recognize that everything I have comes from You; may every blessing be known as a gift from You that others would see You.

REFLECT

Which verse or phrase from the psalm is emphasized in your heart today?

_____

_____

_____

_____

REWRITE

Use phrases from the psalm, prayer or reflection above to write out your prayer to God.

_____

_____

_____

_____

REMEMBER GRATITUDE

Does the psalmist give thanks? If so, for what? If not, why do you think it is left out?

_____

_____

_____

_____

_____

_____

_____

_____

_____

_____

God, be gracious to me and bless me.

REACH FORWARD

Has your prayer ever been so bold as to ask straightforward for God's blessing in your life? What would those blessings look like if you could choose them? The point of this exercise isn't to name your wants from God, but to do a heart check. Would the blessings you would request be gifts that God would love to bless you with?

_____

_____

_____

_____

_____

A PRAYER FOR GOD'S PRESENCE

Day 10

READ

Psalm 61:1-8

PRAY

God, hear me once again. I'm asking You to listen to me. I'm at my wit's end and my heart has grown weak. I need You to lead me to a place of safety. You are my Refuge, the place I run to when the enemy chases me. Protect me, Father. My heart's desire is to live with You forever and I want to take refuge in You. You've heard my promises to you, Lord, and you have given me the heritage of those who fear your name. Keep me in Your presence forever and protect me with Your love and faithfulness. I will sing Your praise forever and keep my promises to You, Lord.

REFLECT

Which verse or phrase from the psalm is emphasized in your heart today?

_____

_____

_____

_____

REWRITE

Use phrases from the psalm, prayer or reflection above to write out your prayer to God.

_____

_____

_____

_____

REMEMBER GRATITUDE

Does the psalmist give thanks? If so, for what? If not, why do you think it is left out?

_____

_____

_____

_____

_____

_____

_____

_____

_____

Lord, You are my Refuge.

REACH FORWARD

David moves from begging God to listen to his prayer to exclaiming the safety he finds in God alone. In verses 3&5, the secret to his shift in thought process is revealed. He remembers that God HAS BEEN his refuge. and God HAS HEARD his vows. If He has done it before, He can do it again! What has God performed in your life that you need Him to do again?

_____

_____

_____

_____

_____

A PRAYER OF HONESTY

Day 11

READ

Psalm 17:1-9

PRAY

Lord, hear my prayer from honest lips. Let any vindication needed come from You; let Your eyes see my integrity. I have not planned evil and I have not sinned with my lips. Though I've been tempted, I have not given in to the ways of the enemy. Lord, I have kept Your commandments and my steps have held to Your paths. I'm praying to You, Lord, because I know that You will answer me. Show me the wonders of Your great love and keep me as the apple of Your eye. Hide me in the shadow of Your wings, away from my enemies.

REFLECT

Which verse or phrase from the psalm is emphasized in your heart today?

_____

_____

_____

_____

REWRITE

Use phrases from the psalm, prayer or reflection above to write out your prayer to God.

_____

_____

_____

_____

REMEMBER GRATITUDE

Does the psalmist give thanks? If so, for what? If not, why do you think it is left out?

_____

_____

_____

_____

_____

_____

_____

_____

_____

Lord, keep me as the apple of Your eye.

REACH FORWARD

David came before the Lord with a clean conscience in this particular prayer. Though he faced temptation and people tried to bring him down, he kept his eyes on the Lord.. Imagine the comfort he took in being so close to the Lord. "in the shadow of His wings!" What do you think Daivd means by "keep m the apple of Your eye?" How could you position yourself as such?

_____

_____

_____

_____

_____

A PRAYER FOR STRENGTH

Day 12

READ

Psalm 28:1-9

PRAY

Lord, I pray to You, my Rock. I need You to not only hear me, but speak to me. I don't want to be like those who sink into the pit of life. Please hear my call for help and respond in Your mercy. Don't let me be a part of those who do evil or speak cordially but have malicious hearts. May those who have no regard for You reap what they have sown. I praise You Lord because You have heard my cry for mercy. You are my strength and my shield. My heart trusts in You, my help. I am full of joy and praise for You are my strength and my fortress. Be my shepherd and carry me, Jesus.

REFLECT

Which verse or phrase from the psalm is emphasized in your heart today?

_____

_____

_____

_____

REWRITE

Use phrases from the psalm, prayer or reflection above to write out your prayer to God.

_____

_____

_____

_____

REMEMBER GRATITUDE

Does the psalmist give thanks? If so, for what? If not, why do you think it is left out?

_____

_____

_____

_____

_____

_____

_____

_____

_____

_____

Praise You, Lord, for being my Strength, my Fortress, and my Shepherd.

REACH FORWARD

David found strength in God alone. God heard his prayers and answered them, providing mercy and protection in his time of need. Since David found the strength he needed to keep going, his praise is abundant throughout his prayer. When have you found God to be your strength? Share those moments with someone to provide encouragement!

_____

_____

_____

_____

_____

A PRAYER OF CONFESSION

Day 13

READ

Psalm 51:1-9

PRAY

Have mercy on me, God. May Your unfailing love and compassion pour over me and cover my sin. Wash my transgressions away. I cannot stop thinking about what I have done. I'm so sorry that I have failed You, Lord. I need You to cleanse my heart; I know that Your forgiveness makes me as white as snow. I have been in such anguish over disappointing you, Lord, that I can't wait to hear happiness once more. While my bones have been crushed, let me rejoice that You love me so much that You correct me. Hide my sin from Your face and forgive my iniquity.

REFLECT

Which verse or phrase from the psalm is emphasized in your heart today?

_____

_____

_____

_____

REWRITE

Use phrases from the psalm, prayer or reflection above to write out your prayer to God.

_____

_____

_____

_____

REMEMBER GRATITUDE

Does the psalmist give thanks? If so, for what? If not, why do you think it is left out?

_____

_____

_____

_____

_____

_____

_____

_____

_____

_____

Lord, forgive me.

REACH FORWARD

Psalm 51 is known as the prayer of David after he had committed adultery with Bathsheba. His agony and regret can be felt in the tone of this psalm. Take a few moments to read 2 Samuel 11 today. How could David have prevented the temptation he fell into? What parameters or guidelines could you implement to prevent situations of enticement from occurring?

_____

_____

_____

_____

_____

A PRAYER FROM BROKENNESS

Day 14

READ

Psalm 51:10-19

PRAY

God, create a clean heart in me. Renew my spirit according to Your way. Please don't let sin separate me from Your presence. I need Your Holy Spirit to restore me. Bring back the joy of knowing You personally and keep me from sin so that I can be an example. Lord, I know I'm guilty of having blood on my hands. I need Your deliverance. I can't speak unless You bring the words. If You bring the words, I will praise You. I know that any work I would try to do to make up for what I have done is not what You desire. Sacrifices are not what You want from me. Lord, I am broken and give my brokenness to You. I know that You love me and that in Your timing, blessing will result from brokenness.

REFLECT

Which verse or phrase from the psalm is emphasized in your heart today?

_____

_____

_____

_____

REWRITE

Use phrases from the psalm, prayer or reflection above to write out your prayer to God.

_____

_____

_____

_____

REMEMBER GRATITUDE

Does the psalmist give thanks? If
so, for what? If not, why do you
think it is left out?

_____

_____

_____

_____

_____

_____

_____

_____

_____

_____

*Lord, bring blessing
from brokenness.*

REACH FORWARD

Yesterday we began reading the back story of Psalm 51. Take a few
moments to read 2 Samuel 12 today. What was David's logic in his
season of mourning? How could you begin to see beauty in your sorrow?
What blessings have resulted from the difficult spaces of your life?

_____

_____

_____

_____

_____

A PRAYER FOR REFUGE

Day 15

READ

Psalm 31:1-5

PRAY

Lord, I take refuge in You. Keep me from doing anything that isn't pleasing to You. Keep me from bringing any shame to Your name. When I am tempted, deliver me through Your righteousness. Lord, listen to me and come to me quickly. I need You to be my rock of refuge. I run to You as my fortress. For Your name's sake, lead me and guide me. Keep me from the enticement the enemy sets out for me. I commit my spirit into Your hands, Lord. Deliver me for You are my faithful God.

REFLECT

Which verse or phrase from the psalm is emphasized in your heart today?

_____

_____

_____

_____

REWRITE

Use phrases from the psalm, prayer or reflection above to write out your prayer to God.

_____

_____

_____

_____

REMEMBER GRATITUDE

Does the psalmist give thanks? If so, for what? If not, why do you think it is left out?

_____

_____

_____

_____

_____

_____

_____

_____

_____

_____

* *

Deliver me, Lord,
in Your faithfulness.

* *

REACH FORWARD

David runs to the Lord for refuge in Psalm 31. He asks for leadership and guidance. He commits himself to the Lord fully. How could you follow his example today that would set the tone for your life choices tomorrow?

_____

_____

_____

_____

_____

A PRAYER FOR SAFETY

Day 16

READ

Psalm 141:1-10

PRAY

Lord, I cry out to You. Come to me quickly and hear me. I place my prayer before You like sweet-smelling perfume on the altar. I lift my hands upward to You in willingness and surrender. Lord, keep me from saying anything I shouldn't. Don't let anything enter and exit my lips without the filter of Your Spirit. Guard my heart from wickedness and make me aware of anything that I should not be a part of. Help me to accept criticism from godly people and continue to shun those who do not serve You. Lord, my eyes are focused on You. Keep me safe from anything that would trap me into evil. Lord, preserve me in safety.

REFLECT

Which verse or phrase from the psalm is emphasized in your heart today?

_____

_____

_____

_____

REWRITE

Use phrases from the psalm, prayer or reflection above to write out your prayer to God.

_____

_____

_____

_____

REMEMBER GRATITUDE

Does the psalmist give thanks? If so, for what? If not, why do you think it is left out?

_____

_____

_____

_____

_____

_____

_____

_____

_____

Father, protect me from enemies, both within and without.

REACH FORWARD

David's words in Psalm 141 request urgent protection and safety. Perhaps he was on the run from his enemies as he penned these lyrics or maybe he was in hiding. Either way, there's a "but." "But my eyes are fixed on You." David did not allow his circumstances to sway his focus. How could you follow his example and realign your vision with the one God has for you?

_____

_____

_____

_____

A PRAYER OF RECOLLECTION

Day 17

READ

Psalm 116:1-7

PRAY

Lord, I love You for hearing my prayer. You know who I am when I call to You because You recognize my voice. I know that You are listening and for this reason, I will call on You as long as I live. Death drew near to me and I stared at the grave; distress and sorrow overcame my soul. In that moment, I called to You, "Lord, save me!" And You did. You are so gracious and compassionate. You have protected me and saved me when I was in difficult places. Lord, You bring rest to my soul because You are good to me.

REFLECT

Which verse or phrase from the psalm is emphasized in your heart today?

_____

_____

_____

_____

REWRITE

Use phrases from the psalm, prayer or reflection above to write out your prayer to God.

_____

_____

_____

_____

REMEMBER GRATITUDE

Does the psalmist give thanks? If
so, for what? If not, why do you
think it is left out?

_____

_____

_____

_____

_____

_____

_____

_____

_____

_____

_____

*Lord, I remember
Your goodness.*

REACH FORWARD

The psalmist begins with beautiful words, "I love the Lord, for he heard
my cry." He then declares that because he knows that God is ever-
listening and always-hearing, he will call on Him as long as he lives. When
was the last time looked back on what God has done in your life and
praised Him for it? It would be a great day to remind God that you plan
on loving Him for as long as he lives.!

_____

_____

_____

_____

A PRAYER FOR SLEEPLESS NIGHTS

Day 18

READ

Psalm 77:1-12

PRAY

God, I cry out to You for help. I need You to hear me. I am lying here in distress, weary, yet unable to sleep. I need Your comfort. Lord, I can barely make out the words to talk to You. I try to focus on Your promises but I can't. I'm lying here wide awake and I can't string two words together to form a sentence. But I remember previously when I asked all the hard questions, "Where are you, God? When are You going to show up? Where is Your mercy? Have I angered You, Lord?" When that happened, I stopped and focused on what You've done for me. I think of the miracles You've worked in my life. And rather than lie here focusing on this present hard space, I will reflect on Your incredible blessings.

REFLECT

Which verse or phrase from the psalm is emphasized in your heart today?

_____

_____

_____

_____

REWRITE

Use phrases from the psalm, prayer or reflection above to write out your prayer to God.

_____

_____

_____

_____

REMEMBER GRATITUDE

Does the psalmist give thanks? If so, for what? If not, why do you think it is left out?

_____

_____

_____

_____

_____   *Lord, comfort me.*

_____

_____

_____

_____

_____

REACH FORWARD

Asaph's thought pattern is the perfect picture of sleepless nights. Until you read verse 10. A pivotal change takes place. Check out the word, "then..." In the midst of restless, troubled thoughts, Asaph takes a turn. It hasn't always been this way; instead of focusing on this present trouble, he chooses to count his blessings. What blessings could you thank God for today?

_____

_____

_____

_____

_____

A PRAYER OF VICTORY

Day 19

READ

Psalm 18:1-6

PRAY

I love you, Lord. You are my strength. You never leave me; I can always run to You. You've saved me from sin and from myself. Your power protects me and keeps me safe. You are worthy of all the praise; thank You for saving me from the enemy. I have seen death and destruction up close and personal. The enemy wants to end my effectiveness, even my life. But no matter how distressed I am, You are near. Lord, I cry out to You for help and I know You hear me. There is no "If you are listening, Lord." I know You are listening. Because You've heard me before and I know You'll answer again.

REFLECT

Which verse or phrase from the psalm is emphasized in your heart today?

_____

_____

_____

_____

REWRITE

Use phrases from the psalm, prayer or reflection above to write out your prayer to God.

_____

_____

_____

_____

REMEMBER GRATITUDE

Does the psalmist give thanks? If so, for what? If not, why do you think it is left out?

_____

_____

_____

_____

_____

_____

_____

_____

_____

Father, You've done it before;
I know You'll do it again.

REACH FORWARD

Psalm 18 is a psalm of David and one of my very favorites. Challenge yourself today to read the entire Psalm and then meditate on verses 46-50. What kind of victory do you need in your own life right now? Give God praise for his unfailing love to You and for how He has worked in your life presently. Then praise Him for what He will do in the future because He is Your good, reliable, loving God.

_____

_____

_____

_____

_____

A PRAYER OF DESPERATION

Day 20

READ

Psalm 102:1-17

PRAY

Lord, I need You to hear me and hear me now. I am so stressed. Please, turn to me and draw me close to listen to my heart. I need answers. The days are passing without purpose and the pain is overwhelming. It feels as though my heart is barely beating and I can't eat. I've lost so much. I'm scraping by in the middle of this desperate space. I can't sleep and I'm so lonely, Lord. I'm sorry for my sin and my failures. Life is passing by without purpose. But God, I know You are in control. I know You have a plan and a purpose. I need You to fulfill Your promises. Show up in all Your glory. Rebuild what has been torn apart. I know You hear and will answer.

REFLECT

Which verse or phrase from the psalm is emphasized in your heart today?

_____

_____

_____

_____

REWRITE

Use phrases from the psalm, prayer or reflection above to write out your prayer to God.

_____

_____

_____

_____

REMEMBER GRATITUDE

Does the psalmist give thanks? If
so, for what? If not, why do you
think it is left out?

_____

_____

_____

_____

_____

_____

_____

_____

_____

* * * * * * * * * * * * * * * * * * * *

*Lord, I'm desperate.
Let it be for You.*

* * * * * * * * * * * * * * * * * * * *

REACH FORWARD

Whether this psalm is hitting you where you live today or not, desperate
times call for desperate measures. Stress-filled living is best navigated as
prayer-filled living. What is the best way for you to remember to turn to
prayer in your deepest moments of distress? Write the word "pray" on a
post-it note and place it where you need the reminder.

_____

_____

_____

_____

_____

A PRAYER OF HOPE

Day 21

READ

Psalm 130:1-8

PRAY

Lord, I need Your help in this deep space. Hear me and bring mercy to me. Thank You for not keeping a record of my mistakes. Thank You for forgiving me. I look to You with reverence and long to serve You fully. So while I am waiting for You to move and provide an answer, my hope is in You. Your Word has never failed and it is the only safe place for my hope to rest. You have never failed me and Your goal is always redemption. Redeem this situation, Father. I look forward eagerly to what You will do to turn this loss into Your glory.

REFLECT

Which verse or phrase from the psalm is emphasized in your heart today?

_____

_____

_____

_____

REWRITE

Use phrases from the psalm, prayer or reflection above to write out your prayer to God.

_____

_____

_____

_____

REMEMBER GRATITUDE

Does the psalmist give thanks? If so, for what? If not, why do you think it is left out?

_____

_____

_____

_____

_____

_____

_____

_____

_____

_____

* * * * * * * * * * * * * * * * * * * *

*My hope is in You
while I wait, Lord.*

* * * * * * * * * * * * * * * * * * * *

REACH FORWARD

Psalm 130 is a song that the children of Israel sang as they journeyed to Jerusalem to worship in the temple. It begins in desperation, moves to forgiveness, and transitions to wait. Is that a cycle you can see in your life? Wishing God would answer, asking Him to forgive You for doubting, and then waiting on Him to work? In that place is where hope must rest in His promises. Have you placed your hope in God's promises today? How could you do that right now?

_____

_____

_____

_____

_____

A PRAYER FOR SOLUTIONS

Day 22

READmark

Psalm 54:1-7

PRAY

God, I need You to save me for Your name's sake. Through Your power, vindicate the evil lurking. Lord, please hear me. I am under full attack from the enemy who wants me dead. He has no regard for You, Lord. I know You are my help and the only One who can keep me going. in Your faithfulness, destroy the works of the enemy. I praise Your name for it is good, faithful and true. I know You don't just have the solutions for my problems; You are the solution to my problems. Give me the strength to look forward to celebrating Your triumphs.

REFLECT

Which verse or phrase from the psalm is emphasized in your heart today?

_____

_____

_____

_____

REWRITE

Use phrases from the psalm, prayer or reflection above to write out your prayer to God.

_____

_____

_____

_____

REMEMBER GRATITUDE

Does the psalmist give thanks? If so, for what? If not, why do you think it is left out?

_____
_____
_____
_____
_____
_____
_____
_____
_____
_____

* *

Lord, be my answer.

* *

REACH FORWARD

David was in hiding when he wrote this song of praise. Imagine the fear that haunted him. Imagine the anger and rage of the enemy so thick it could be felt in the air. While David doesn't know the answer to solving his problems, he knows to look to the Lord not for his answer, but as his answer. Do you see the difference? Explain it in your own words below. How could you embrace David's attitude?

_____
_____
_____
_____
_____

A PRAYER OF SURRENDER

Day 23

READ

Psalm 84:1-12

PRAY

Lord, it is so good to be close to You. My soul longs to not only be near Your presence, but near to Your heart. I don't want to live at a distance from You, but I want to offer myself to You in full surrender. I want to live as a channel of Your love. I know that this is a beautiful way to live and I choose it as a path of praise. I need Your strength for the journey; let me rely on You from day to day, moment by moment. Let me live for Your glory and walk with integrity before You. You are the Light and Shield of my life. I know that all blessings come from you. Help me to place every ounce of my trust in You alone.

REFLECT

Which verse or phrase from the psalm is emphasized in your heart today?

_____

_____

_____

_____

REWRITE

Use phrases from the psalm, prayer or reflection above to write out your prayer to God.

_____

_____

_____

_____

REMEMBER GRATITUDE

Does the psalmist give thanks? If so, for what? If not, why do you think it is left out?

_____

_____

_____

_____

_____

_____

_____

_____

_____

_____

* * * * * * * * * * * * * * * * * * * *

Lord, I give myself to You.

* * * * * * * * * * * * * * * * * * * *

REACH FORWARD

Korah, the author of Psalm 84, compares his closeness to God with physical places in the temple. He mentions being in the house of the Lord, then he discusses the courts of the Lord, and finally, he mentions the altar. These physical places are spiritual comparisons of personal relationship with God. How would you explain them? At which place do you see yourself?

_____

_____

_____

_____

_____

A PRAYER AGAINST THE ENEMY

Day 24

READ

Psalm 64:1-10

PRAY

God, I complain to You. Protect me from the enemy. There's a lot going on and I feel certain that I don't even know the half of it. Harsh words have been spoken. Although I have not done anything to provoke them, the enemy longs to take me down and sometimes he uses people to do that. I know there is evil being plotted against me because Your enemy is after Your child. Lord, You know his plans and I pray that You thwart them. Do not allow him to have the victory. Let others see the power You have and wonder at Your works. Give them something to talk about. I rejoice in You as my Refuge. May You receive all the glory.

REFLECT

Which verse or phrase from the psalm is emphasized in your heart today?

_____

_____

_____

_____

REWRITE

Use phrases from the psalm, prayer or reflection above to write out your prayer to God.

_____

_____

_____

_____

REMEMBER GRATITUDE

Does the psalmist give thanks? If
so, for what? If not, why do you
think it is left out?

_____

_____

_____

_____

_____

_____

_____

_____

*Lord, give them something to
talk about.*

REACH FORWARD

David sat in the middle of a conspiracy when he penned the lyrics to
Psalm 64. It was an ugly situation with sharp words and premeditated
acts. The song begins in desperation, but moves to faith in God's power.
Have you witnessed a situation that took a swift turn from despair to
God's glory? How can you give God glory for it right now?

_____

_____

_____

_____

_____

A PRAYER OF REJECTION

Day 25

READ

Psalm 88:1-9

PRAY

Lord, You are my God. You have saved me and I don't know what else to do but come to You. I'm overwhelmed and drawing near death. It seems I could be counted as one who is dead. I have no strength and am as lifeless as those who lie in the grave. God, I don't want to be where You have me right now. This situation is too much for me and I feel Your anger. I've lost friends and now they hate me. I've been completely rejected. I'm stuck in a hard place with no way out. Lord, I'm calling out to You. I open my hands to You, ready to receive what You have for me.

REFLECT

Which verse or phrase from the psalm is emphasized in your heart today?

_____

_____

_____

_____

REWRITE

Use phrases from the psalm, prayer or reflection above to write out your prayer to God.

_____

_____

_____

_____

REMEMBER GRATITUDE

Does the psalmist give thanks? If
so, for what? If not, why do you
think it is left out?

_____

_____

_____

_____

_____

*Lord, receive me
in a place of rejection.*

_____

_____

_____

_____

REACH FORWARD

Hernan the Ezrahite wrote Psalm 88, a maskil of deepest sorrow. In the
portion for today's reading, His feelings of overwhelm seem rooted in
rejection. Is this true for you? Have you ever found that one of the
reasons you feel overwhelmed is because you've felt the sting of
rejection? What if you opened your hands to receive what God has for
you in this moment? How could you word that prayer? Hint: Check out
the remainder of Psalm 88.

_____

_____

_____

_____

_____

A PRAYER OF GLORY

Day 26

READ

Psalm 86:1-10

PRAY

God, I need You to hear me. And not only hear me, but answer me. I've been faithful to You; guard my life. I trust in You; You are my God. I need Your mercy every moment of every day. Bring joy to my heart, Lord. I know that You forgive and that You love me. Hear my prayer for mercy. I'm disappointed and disillusioned, so I'm calling to You, the One who answers. There is no one like You, God. No one can do what You do. I worship You and give You glory for Your greatness. You do incredible, beyond-my-imagination things and I'm so grateful.

REFLECT

Which verse or phrase from the psalm is emphasized in your heart today?

_____

_____

_____

_____

REWRITE

Use phrases from the psalm, prayer or reflection above to write out your prayer to God.

_____

_____

_____

_____

REMEMBER GRATITUDE

Does the psalmist give thanks? If so, for what? If not, why do you think it is left out?

_____

_____

_____

_____

_____

_____

_____

_____

_____

There is no one like You, God..

REACH FORWARD

David's honesty and love for the Lord shines in Psalm 86. The blend of his heartfelt words is beautiful and God-honoring. His prayer focus in this psalm is giving God the glory He deserves. What words could you pen that would give God praise for Who He is and what He does?

_____

_____

_____

_____

_____

A PRAYER FROM THE HEART

Day 27

READ

Psalm 86:11-17

PRAY

Lord, I need You to teach me how I should live. Show me Your faithfulness to make daily decisions. Keep my heart focused on You, respecting Who you are. I give You all the praise, Lord, with everything in me. I glorify Your name forever. You have loved me with love incomprehensible. You have pulled me out of discouragement, distress, despair and depression. No matter what others throw my way, You are compassionate and gracious. You are patient towards me, loving me always, and faithful in that love. Lord, reveal to me what You are doing. Let Your glory be known through a sign of your goodness. You are my help and comfort and I praise You.

REFLECT

Which verse or phrase from the psalm is emphasized in your heart today?

_____

_____

_____

_____

REWRITE

Use phrases from the psalm, prayer or reflection above to write out your prayer to God.

_____

_____

_____

_____

REMEMBER GRATITUDE

Does the psalmist give thanks? If so, for what? If not, why do you think it is left out?

_____

_____

_____

_____

_____

_____

_____

_____

_____

_____

Teach me Your way, Lord.

REACH FORWARD

In the second half of Psalm 86, David asks for wisdom and gives praise to the Lord. In verse 16, David shares a hint of how he has learned to walk with the Lord faithfully. He states that his mother was his example of the faith. Have you ever pondered how she must have influenced him? Who could you list in your life as a precious example of faith? Thank God for him or her in the space below.

_____

_____

_____

_____

_____

A PRAYER OF CONFIDENCE

Day 28

READ

Psalm 119:145-149

PRAY

Lord, I call to you from the deepest parts of my heart. I want to obey Your Word. I long to be close to You; I want to keep Your Word, just as You keep Your promises. I want to wake up with You on my heart. Let my first morning act to be placing my hope in You. When I can't sleep, place Your promises in my thoughts. I need You to hear my voice in Your love. Preserve me, Lord and keep me focused on honoring You. Your Word is true and I have learned that they are eternal promises. You have set up Your Word to last forever and I praise You for it.

REFLECT

Which verse or phrase from the psalm is emphasized in your heart today?

_____

_____

_____

_____

REWRITE

Use phrases from the psalm, prayer or reflection above to write out your prayer to God.

_____

_____

_____

_____

REMEMBER GRATITUDE

Does the psalmist give thanks? If so, for what? If not, why do you think it is left out?

_____

_____

_____

_____

_____

_____

_____

_____

_____

_____

Lord, keep my heart aligned with Your Word.

REACH FORWARD

Psalm 119:145-152 is a declaration of truth. It is a confident prayer, grounded on the principle that God's Word never changes and the truth of His promises can always be counted on. What are the things that cause you to allow doubt to creep in your relationship with the Lord? What are some practical things you could do in order to squelch doubt at the first sign? (Hint: Verse 148.)

_____

_____

_____

_____

_____

A PRAYER FOR RELIEF

Day 29

READ

Psalm 6:1-10

PRAY

Lord, don't be angry with me. I need Your mercy because I'm completely exhausted. Heal me, Lord; the pain has seeped into my bones. The anguish is deep and I keep wondering how much longer it's going to last. Deliver me through Your unfailing love. I can't praise You if I'm in the grave. I've exhausted myself with grief. The tears can't be stopped in the night. I can't see clearly through the tears. Lord, I know that You take me as I am, sorrow and all. Let the enemy be put to shame because You answer my prayer.

REFLECT

Which verse or phrase from the psalm is emphasized in your heart today?

_____

_____

_____

_____

REWRITE

Use phrases from the psalm, prayer or reflection above to write out your prayer to God.

_____

_____

_____

_____

REMEMBER GRATITUDE

Does the psalmist give thanks? If so, for what? If not, why do you think it is left out?

_____

_____

_____

_____

_____

Father,
deliver me.

_____

_____

_____

_____

REACH FORWARD

By now you may have noticed a theme in David's prayers. His depth of emotion holds true whether in sorrow in joy. His direct honesty with God is never held back and no matter how he is feeling, he trusts God with his emotions. Have you ever been tempted not to pray because you think God wouldn't want to hear your prayer? What could you learn from Psalm 6 in regards to that thought?

_____

_____

_____

_____

_____

A PRAYER FROM THE DARK

Day 30

READ

Psalm 142:1-7

PRAY

Lord, I am crying out for Your mercy. I can't say the words quickly enough to explain all that is going wrong. I'm in trouble and I'm afraid. Lord, I know You see me and I know that You are watching over me but I feel abandoned. No one is close to me; no one cares. I don't have anyone I can run to. Except there is You. Oh, God, thank You for being the One I can run to. I am desperate and I need You to win over the enemy. Those against me are too strong for me. I'm in a prison, Lord, and it is not of my own making. Set me free so I can praise You. Let my life be a testimony of Your goodness to me.

REFLECT

Which verse or phrase from the psalm is emphasized in your heart today?

_____

_____

_____

_____

REWRITE

Use phrases from the psalm, prayer or reflection above to write out your prayer to God.

_____

_____

_____

_____

REMEMBER GRATITUDE

Does the psalmist give thanks? If so, for what? If not, why do you think it is left out?

_____

_____

_____

_____

_____

_____

_____

_____

_____

_____

Father,
free me from the dark.

REACH FORWARD

David's prayer in Psalm 142 was written while he was in a cave. No doubt, in hiding, his plea for light at the end of the tunnel was warranted. He bluntly states that no one cares. But just as quickly as he declares it, he turns to God in prayer, as if to say, "But I know You care." Take a walk in nature today and make some detailed observations. Maybe the color of the sky or the shade of the leaves. Whatever it is, note below how nature reveals God's care for you.

_____

_____

_____

_____

_____

A PRAYER FOR DELIVERANCE

Day 31

READ

Psalm 3:1-8

PRAY

Lord, I have a lot of enemies. Whether situations, circumstances, disease, or depression, the issues are mounting taller than me. It doesn't look like You are near and others might see me and think that I'm a goner. But I know You are my shield. You are the One who lifts up my head when I'm discouraged. You are the One who answers me from heaven. I can sleep at night because You sustain me. No matter how many enemies I have, no matter how many issues befall me, I know I don't have to be afraid. God, deliver me for I know that true deliverance comes only from You. Bless me. Bless your people.

REFLECT

Which verse or phrase from the psalm is emphasized in your heart today?

_____

_____

_____

_____

REWRITE

Use phrases from the psalm, prayer or reflection above to write out your prayer to God.

_____

_____

_____

_____

REMEMBER GRATITUDE

Does the psalmist give thanks? If so, for what? If not, why do you think it is left out?

_____

_____

_____

_____

_____

_____

_____

_____

_____

_____

Lord,
deliver me.

REACH FORWARD

Psalm 3 was written when David was running away from his son, Absalom, who wanted to kill him. Imagine the heartache of having a son who wants you dead and is willing to do it himself. Yet David declares that no matter how many enemies he has, even when it is his own son, his trust remains in God. He believes in the One who has delivered him before. What do you need delivered from today? Be encouraged; no matter how low the trouble, God has the power to deliver you.

_____

_____

_____

_____

_____

You did it!

CONGRATULATIONS

Rachel Wojo hosts Bible reading challenges on her popular blog, rachelwojo.com, which rallies readers of all ages to search God's Word for solutions to life's problems. Her site has over 30,000 subscribers, and her six-week Bible reading plan for children is used by more than four million people worldwide. Rachel is the author of One More Step: Finding Strength When You Feel Like Giving Up. She is also a public speaker and contributes monthly articles for well-known faith-based companies. Rachel and her husband, Matt, reside in Ohio and are the parents of seven children.

Find more at
rachelwojo.com/shop

Made in United States
Orlando, FL
10 December 2024

55294280R00041